T0195658

YOU'RE GOLDEN

GOLDEN

JOURNAL

A COMPREHENSIVE GUIDE FOR
SELF-DISCOVERY AND DIRECTION
SO YOU CAN SHINE

KAY BOYER

BALBOA.PRESS
A DIVISION OF HAY HOUSE

Balboa Press books may be ordered through booksellers or by contacting:

Balboa Press
A Division of Hay House
1663 Liberty Drive
Bloomington, IN 47403
www.balboapress.com
844-682-1282

Print information available on the last page.

ISBN: 978-1-9822-7442-9 (sc)
ISBN: 978-1-9822-7443-6 (hc)
ISBN: 978-1-9822-7451-1 (e)

Balboa Press rev. date: 09/16/2021

She was like the sun,

She knew her place in the world -

She would shine again regardless

of all the storms and changeable weather

She wouldn't adjust her purpose

for things that pass.

NIKKI ROWE

A NOTE FROM THE AUTHOR

Hello, my name is Kay and I am a hopeless believer that everyone can find their own version of happiness. For myself, it took years of therapy, inner-work, tears, courage and growth, but it worked. So, I collected all of the concepts that I learned and put them into a journal to help you find your own version of happiness.

My current life's motto: Live a life of value. Take responsibility. Help others. Be open. Be present. Require more of yourself. Require less of yourself, give yourself grace. Be aware of what triggers your emotions. Listen to your intuition. Work with who you really are. Find support. Find love. Find the good. Have boundaries. Live with courage and purpose. Get stronger. Contribute relentlessly.
Be brave. Be love. Value yourself. Value others. Be grateful.

With love,

Kay

And a thank you to my support system through my life.
Here's to the people who didn't even know that they helped my soul for the better: Stewart, Morgan, Kate, Jess, Karen, Mallory, Marie, Lacy, Stacia, Cara, Jill, Elanie, Kevin, Roslyn, Everett, and Hannah L. Thank you for being you, so I could be a better me. I see you.

[Journal designed by Hannah Liddell of Beyond the Treetops | Creative Media]

INTRODUCTION

You're Golden Journal will give you a chance to ponder the questions of what you actually want and what actually matters to you. It then helps you to guide your future accordingly.

Take the time. Ask the questions. Evaluate your life.
Do the work. Live your Golden life.

HOW TO DO THE YOU'RE GOLDEN JOURNAL

Find a quiet space and a pen.

Go through the journal page by page, filling out the questions in order. Feel free to go back and add any comments in past sections as new thoughts come up.

Progress through the journal as quickly or as slowly as you like.

Make a plan to meet your goals.

Follow the plan.

Meet your goals.

+ Bonus questions in the back section of the book that can be filled out anytime.
+ Pages for extra journaling or mapping your goals in the back section as well.

Always answer from a place of love and understanding.
Be honest. Be open. Be willing. Show up for yourself.
Make the changes. Be Golden.

++++ MENTAL HEALTH DISCLAIMER ++++

+ This journal is not to replace advice from a mental health professional. If you feel any overwhelming negative thoughts or emotions, consult a professional therapist, psychologist, doctor or counselor.

+ This journal is not designed as a treatment for individuals experiencing a mental health condition. Nothing in this journal should be viewed as a substitute for professional advice.

TABLE OF CONTENTS

SELF-AWARENESS

Just living is not enough…

One must have sunshine,

freedom, and a little flower.

HANS CHRISTIAN ANDERSEN

EXPLORE YOUR INNER SELF.
BEGIN FROM A PLACE OF
LOVE AND ACCEPTANCE.

LIFE INVENTORY

How would you describe these areas of your life?
Comment on your satisfaction in each box.
Which could use growth?

HAPPINESS + HOPE	RELATIONSHIPS + LOVE FOR OTHERS	CHARACTER + VIRTUE + HONOR	ADVENTURE + CURIOSITY + CHALLENGE
○ Needs Growth	○ Needs Growth	○ Needs Growth	○ Needs Growth
PURPOSE + CONTRIBUTION	PHYSICAL HEALTH	MENTAL HEALTH	SHAME + GUILT + REGRET
○ Needs Growth	○ Needs Growth	○ Needs Growth	○ Needs Growth
GROWTH + LEARNING	FINANCIAL MANAGEMENT + TIME MANAGEMENT	MATURITY + RESPONSIBILITIES	SPIRITUALITY
○ Needs Growth	○ Needs Growth	○ Needs Growth	○ Needs Growth
STRESS LEVELS	COMMUNITY + SUPPORT	BOUNDARIES	SELF-CARE + SELF-ESTEEM
○ Needs Growth	○ Needs Growth	○ Needs Growth	○ Needs Growth

What parts of your life are you satisfied with?

_____

_____

_____

_____

What parts of your life are you not satisfied with?

_____

_____

_____

_____

What roles do you have in life?

_____

_____

_____

_____

Who are you beyond your roles?

_____

_____

_____

_____

What do you care about most in life?

_____

_____

_____

_____

PURPOSE

RALPH WALDO EMERSON SAID, *"The purpose of life is not to be happy. It is to be useful, to be honorable, to be compassionate, to have it make some difference that you lived and lived well."*

What do you believe the purpose of life to be?

1. What makes life worth living to you?

VALUES

What do you value? Why?

_____

_____

_____

_____

What do you think contributes to a life well lived?

_____

_____

_____

_____

A highly developed values system is like a compass.
It serves as a guide to point you
in the right direction when you are lost.

IDOWU KOYENIKAN

JOY AND FULFILLMENT

We cannot cure the world of sorrows,
but we can choose to live in joy.

JOSEPH CAMPBELL

What brightens your world?

What makes time fly by?

What in life do you
look forward to?

What gives you joy?

SELF-DISCOVERY

It takes courage … to endure the sharp pains of
self-discovery rather than choose to
take the dull pain of unconsciousness that
would last the rest of our lives.

MARIANNE WILLIAMSON

Where do you struggle in life?

Where do you feel in need?

Where do you feel empty?

When and where are you not your best self?

How can you get help from others or growth
from yourself to manage your struggles?

When are you the
most happy?

How can you feel fulfilled?

When are you the
most happy?

Where can you find
fulfilments for your
needs in healthy ways?

When and where are you your best self?

Thunderstorms are as much our friends as the sunshine.

CRISS JAMI

SELF-REFLECTION

Your visions will become clear only when you can look into your own heart. Who looks outside, dreams; who looks inside, awakes.

CARL JUNG

What takes away your energy?	What makes you feel energized?

What makes you feel unfulfilled?	What makes you feel fulfilled?

DIG DEEPER

What situations make you feel each way and why?

_____
_____
_____
_____
_____

What changes could you make to your life to help support your need for fulfillment and energy?

_____
_____
_____
_____
_____

Why is it important to guard your own energy and fulfillment?

_____
_____
_____
_____
_____

HABITS

Make hay while the sun shines.

MIGUEL DE CERVANTES

What habits are helping you?

_____

_____

_____

_____

_____

What habits are hindering you?

_____

_____

_____

_____

_____

What actions fill up your daily minutes? Do you use your time well?

_____

_____

_____

_____

_____

How could you set up better boundaries for your habits?

_____

_____

_____

_____

_____

BEST SELF IN
DAY-TO-DAY LIVING

How do you react to stressors when you are at your best?

How do you react to stressors when you are at your worst?

What are ways you could keep yourself in your best-self zone?

Where do you feel like you need to grow?

What will it actually take to make you happy in life?

What do you really want out of life?

What is keeping you from having the life you want?

A flower cannot blossom without sunshine,
and man cannot live without love.

MAX MULLER

FEARS

If you spend your whole life waiting for the storm,
you'll never enjoy the sunshine.

MORRIS WEST

WE ALL HAVE THEM.
WORK TO IDENTIFY
AND NAME THEM.

What are your greatest fears?

When are your fears at their worst?

How can you use your fears to grow?

How can you grow to help manage your fears?

How would your best-self handle those fears?

How would a healthy mentor advise you to grow
through your fears?

Do you have any past traumas that need healed
to help you grow through your fears?

Is there a mentor or a professional who can
assist you in healing?

INSECURITIES

If you want to see the sunshine, you have to weather the storm.

FRANK LANE

EVERYONE HAS THEM.
WORK TO BRING
THEM TO LIGHT.

What are your insecurities?

When are you not your best self?
Answer with self-awareness and acceptance.

How can you use your insecurities to grow,
have compassion, or relate to others?

THOUGHT TENDENCIES

The mind is everything. What you think, you become.

BUDDHA

> BE AWARE OF
> WHAT YOU THINK
> THROUGHOUT YOUR DAY.

What are habitual thoughts that you have throughout your day?

POSITIVE THOUGHTS	NEGATIVE THOUGHTS

How do you cope with stressors in your life?

REPLACEMENT THOUGHTS

Darkness cannot drive out darkness; only light can do that.
Hate cannot drive out hate; only love can do that.

MARTIN LUTHER KING JR.

The human mind has a tendency to focus on the negative aspects of life in order to feel like it can cope with any future threats. How can you work beyond that tendency and train your brain to have courage and be empowered?

REPLACE YOUR NEGATIVE
THOUGHTS WITH
POSITIVE THOUGHTS.

NEGATIVE THOUGHTS ⟶	POSITIVE REPLACEMENT THOUGHTS

HEALING

Courage doesn't happen when you have all the answers.
It happens when you are ready to face the questions you
have been avoiding your whole life.

SHANNON L. ALDER

APPROACH THESE
QUESTIONS WITH
SELF-LOVE AND AWARENESS.

Where do you feel that your life needs healing?

What is a lingering feeling that you need to face?

How can you find healing in healthy ways?

Love comforteth like sunshine after rain.

WILLIAM SHAKESPEARE

Where can you find love, acceptance, and support for any hurt in your life?

_____

_____

_____

_____

What group could you join for support? Who could you ask for help? Is there a mentor who could help you?

_____

_____

_____

_____

How can finding ways to heal yourself help you love yourself and others more?

_____

_____

_____

_____

If you want to shine like a sun, first burn like a sun.

A.P.J. ABDUL KALAM

PEACE

Do you feel at peace with your life and your life's choices, in either the big picture or in any small day-to-day decisions?

Are there any actions you feel you should take to be at peace with yourself?

Is there any support that you need to be able to grow in this area?

How can you bring about a more peaceful and healthy future for you and those around you?

Do you need growth or forgiveness for yourself or others?

Never give up. Today is hard, tomorrow will be worse, but the day after tomorrow will be sunshine.

JACK MA

EMOTIONS

When we understand people; when we understand situations;
when we understand what matters; when we understand
the why's, the what's and the how's; when we understand
the trigger of actions, we least inflict pain on
ourselves and unto others.

ERNEST AGYEMANG YEBOAH

Emotions educate us. Just accept the emotion.
Feel it and try to understand it.

NOTE: For this exercise, emotions by themselves are neither good nor bad.
What is important, is to understand why you are experiencing them, and
being able to have a healthy response and action.

PICK AN EMOTION.

sad	motivated	empty	compassionate
depressed	content	guilty	sensitive
anxious	jealous	annoyed	determined
nervous	volatile	empowered	energetic
irritated	unmotivated	supported	calm
lonely	angry	powerful	amazed
excited	deflated	happy	peaceful
hopeful	tired	grateful	inspired
joyful	fearful	confident	stable
at peace			

Response and Action on the following pages.

What happened to make you feel that way?

What were the circumstances around your situation?

What did your emotions tell you about that situation?

Did you handle your behavior in a mature way after feeling the emotion? Why?

How can you set your life up so that you respond to triggers in healthy ways?

What are needs that you have that this emotion is clueing you into?

Are there any boundaries you could implement?

Are there any mentors you could talk to?

What support do you need to handle this emotion better?

What growth do you need to handle this situation better?

CONCERNING YOUR EMOTIONAL RESPONSE:
Did you do what you felt was right? What was the outcome?

To be happy, you must be your own sunshine.

C.E. JERNINGHAM

+ *Additional Emotions Questions are available in the last section of this journal.*

MOODS

I am not in a bad mood; everyone is just annoying.

UNKNOWN

Seek to gain awareness of your moods.
Moods are part of your emotional rhythm.

+ If you need help managing moods or
feel you have a mood condition, consult a doctor or therapist.

Review the chart below. When do you feel each mood?

ANNOYED / NERVOUS:	EXCITED / HAPPY:
TRIGGERS:	TRIGGERS:
SAD / DEPRESSED:	CONTENT / AT PEACE:
TRIGGERS:	TRIGGERS:

What perceived triggers contribute to you feeling that way?

_____

_____

_____

_____

_____

How can you get support for any perceived struggle with your moods?

_____

_____

_____

_____

What self-care activity might help get your needs met so that you can meet the needs of others?

_____

_____

_____

_____

_____

A cloudy day is no match for a sunny disposition.

WILLIAM ARTHUR WARD

FOOD AND MOOD

Emotions and Mood are affected by many things: hormones, past experiences, subconscious beliefs, brain chemistry, gut health, and so much more, including food.

On this page, notice your bodies reaction to triggering foods. Caffeine, sugar, salty, and/or carbs are some examples of foods to notice.

Use this as a tool to explore this particular contribution to your emothional health. This is only a small portion of what contributes to your overall mood and emotion.

Fill in what you ate of any triggering foods and record how you feel.

FOOD CHOICE	20 MINUTES LATER	1 HOUR LATER	12 HOURS LATER

FOOD CHOICE	20 MINUTES LATER	1 HOUR LATER	12 HOURS LATER

Also notice if a certain feeling triggers you to eat food for comfort. Take note of this reaction and try to replace it with a healthier habit. Here are some good ideas:

Eat something healthy

Take a walk

Meet with a friend

Exercise

Journal

Play music

Draw

Pet a puppy

GROWTH

We all have an unsuspected

reserve of strength inside that

emerges when life puts us to the test.

ISABEL ALLENDE

EXPLORE YOUR LIFE CHOICES
AND OPTIONS FOR MATURITY.
FRAME YOUR ANSWERS
IN THE PERSPECTIVE OF
YOUR BEST SELF.

YOUR STORY

Don't let the shadows of yesterday
spoil the sunshine of tomorrow. Live for today.

JERNINGHAM

What is the story that you want to tell about your life?

Write your story with yourself cast as the hero. Write down
all the aspects that you want your best life to have.

EVERY DAY REFLECTED

After every difficulty, ask yourself two questions:
"What did I do right?" and "What would I do differently?"

BRIAN TRACY

What worked today?

_____

_____

_____

_____

What didn't work today? Why didn't it work?

_____

_____

_____

_____

What changes could you make in the future to help your life and other peoples' lives work better?

_____

_____

_____

_____

LIMITATIONS

Don't let what you cannot do interfere with what you can do.

JOHN R. WOODEN

PERSONAL LIMITATIONS | True or Perceived?

You need to recognize if a limitation is true or only perceived to be true. How can you pivot your actions or beliefs in life to overcome either type?

_____

_____

What are true limitations in your life concerning your growth or happiness?

What are new approaches you could take to work around your true limitations? Are there systems, machines, or other people that can help support your process?

APPROACHES

SUPPORT

When you can't find the sunshine, be the sunshine.

UNKNOWN

What are your perceived
limitations?
Why are they only perceived?

How can you grow beyond
those limiting beliefs?

What are new unlimited
beliefs for your life?
How can you live with
bigger life beliefs + influence
others to do the same?

Are you scared to succeed?
How can you work past
that fear?

EXCUSES

Don't go around saying the world owes you a living.
The world owes you nothing. It was here first.

MARK TWAIN

Have the wisdom to consider your situation with love,
acceptance, understanding, maturity, courage, and strength.

What excuses do you use that cause you to get less in life than
you could have gotten?

What are your life's true challenges that you have to work harder
to overcome?

Where should you give yourself grace, and where should you get
stronger? Do you have the wisdom to know the difference?

Where can you get support?

YOUR WHOLE SELF

*A flower cannot blossom without sunshine,
and man cannot live without love.*

MAX MULLER

Are your human needs being met?

PHYSICAL NEEDS:	SOCIAL NEEDS:
health, safety, movement, nutrition, sleep, shelter, companionship, touch, rest	*healthy relationships, connection and acceptance, companionship, community, giving + receiving love*
MENTAL NEEDS:	**SELF-ESTEEM NEEDS:**
being challenged, growth, adventure, having purpose, financial security	*worthiness, a sense of self-value and/or accomplishment, contribution to others*

Where are your needs not being met?

_____

_____

_____

How can you meet these needs in healthy ways?

PHYSICAL NEEDS: *health, safety, movement, nutrition, sleep, shelter, companionship, touch, rest*	SOCIAL NEEDS: *healthy relationships, connection and acceptance, companionship, community, giving + receiving love*
MENTAL NEEDS: *being challenged, growth, adventure, having purpose, financial security*	SELF-ESTEEM NEEDS: *worthiness, a sense of self-value and/or accomplishment, contribution to others*

Actions I could take to better my life today:

_____

_____

_____

_____

Live in the sunshine, swim the sea, drink the wild air.

RALPH WALDO EMERSON

GRATITUDE

What you focus on grows, what you think about expands, and what you dwell upon determines your destiny.

ROBIN SHARMA

I am grateful for . . .

YOUR TOMBSTONE

Don't be afraid of death, be afraid of the unlived life.

NATALIE BABBITT

Everyone makes some sort of impact on others.

What do you want your tombstone to say about you?

How do you want to be remembered?

What legacy do you want to leave behind?

THE UNIVERSE AND EXISTENCE

*The most important decision we make, is whether
we believe we live in a friendly or a hostile universe.*

ALBERT EINSTEIN

Where did we all come from, and why are we here?
These are the questions that humans have grappled with since
the beginning of time. No pressure. Just dive into what you
think on the matter and be aware of those beliefs.

Your thoughts on this big topic of the universe and existence:

GROWTH

To be mature means to face, and not evade,
every fresh crisis that comes.

FRITZ KUNKEL

You can't control everything that happens to you,
but you can control your reaction and attitude.

What in your life is out of your control that you need to make
peace with?

What in life do you have control over but aren't doing anything
about? Why?

What are things you could do to help yourself grow in that area?

Do you take responsibility for problems, or do you blame others
or life itself? Why?

YOUR FOCUS

Tell me what you pay attention to
and I will tell you who you are.

JOSÉ ORTEGA Y GASSET

What you focus on grows.

What is your mind focusing on?

What can you focus on that is constructive to your life?

How can you keep your attention on the good?
What can you make as a trigger to remind yourself to
focus on a positive aspect of life?

Stop walking through the world looking for confirmation
that you don't belong. You will always find it because
you've made that your mission. Stop scouring people's faces
for evidence that you're not enough. You will always find it
because you've made that your goal.

BRENÉ BROWN

LIFE LESSONS

It's not enough to have lived.
We should be determined to live for something.
May I suggest that it be creating joy for others, sharing
what we have for the betterment of personkind,
bringing hope to the lost and love to the lonely.

LEO BUSCAGLIA

What are the lessons from your life that you want to tell
future generations about how they can have a more fulfilled life?

☐

☐

☐

☐

☐

☐

☐

☐

☐

☐

☐

☐

☐

BEST SELF

Take up one idea. Make that one idea your life – think of it,
dream of it, live on that idea. Let the brain, muscles, nerves,
every part of your body, be full of that idea, and just leave
every other idea alone. This is the way to success,
that is way great spiritual giants are produced.

SWAMI VIVEKANANDA

Dwell on the best version of yourself.

Who is the person you want to become?

_____

How do they act?   What do they care about?

YOU ARE WORTHY

When you recover or discover something that nourishes
your soul and brings joy, care enough about yourself
to make room for it in your life.

JEAN SHINODA BOLEN

Take time every day to love and care for yourself.
Then you are in a better place to love others.

How much time do you take for yourself each day?

What are your self-care activities?

What are self-care activities you want to implement in your daily,
weekly, monthly, and yearly life.

DAILY	WEEKLY	MONTHLY

TIME

Life isn't a matter of milestones, but of moments.

ROSE KENNEDY

Life is every small moment added up. Learn to live in the everyday moments. Have patience.

Do you tend to have your mind in the future, past, or present?

☐ FUTURE   ☐ PAST   ☐ PRESENT

What are your small daily moments adding up to in your life?

Do you have patience? How can you learn to give attention to the present moments without hurrying to the future?

How can you learn to find meaning in the little things of the everyday?

Do you have healing from your past so you can be present and hopeful for a healthy future?

SUPPORT

We are one, after all, you and I,

together we suffer, together exist and

forever will recreate one another.

PIERRE TEILHARD DE CHARDIN

GET SUPPORT. BE SUPPORTIVE
OF YOURSELF AND OTHERS.
LIVE IN LOVE, ACCEPTANCE,
AND COMMUNITY.

SUPPORT SYSTEM

I want to be around people that do things.
I don't want to be around people anymore that judge
or talk about what people do. I want to be around people
that dream and support and do things.

AMY POEHLER

The people around you have an impact on your life.

Is your social system supportive? Do you feel accepted, loved, or valued? Why or why not?

....
....
....
....

Where do you wish you had more support?

....
....
....
....

To love and be loved is to feel the sun from both sides.

DAVID VISCOTT

BOUNDARIES

Each of us has the power to inspire or depress,
to lift others or to push them down.

WILFERD PETERSON

Boundaries are there to protect you.
Boundaries in relationships are a healthy way to
keep your needs and the needs of others in check,
a way for everyone to respect each other.

Do you keep healthy boundaries in your relationships?

Do you keep good boundaries for how others treat you? Do you keep good boundaries for how you treat yourself?

What boundaries do you need to put in place to keep your relationships healthy?

How do you feel when you put a new boundary in place?

Why do you have the boundaries that you have?

Has something in your past informed this behavior?

What is one new boundary you could put into place for each facet of your life?

Inner self: Outer self: With others:
With your emotional or mental state:

What are boundaries that you need to implement that are extra hard and need support?

How are your boundaries concerning:
social media, indulgences, food, drinking, thoughts, emotions, behavior, addictions, laziness, money-spending, relationships, toxic people, etc.

FINDING SUPPORT

Your support network is the solid ground from which you can propel yourself upwards.

ANNA BARNES

Seek healthy groups and mentors.

What new activities could you incorporate into your life to help with your emotional, mental, and social growth?

_____

_____

_____

Following your interests.

What are groups you want to join someday?

_____

_____

_____

Where can you seek mentorships from people you admire?
It can be as simple as having coffee with an elderly person you admire or starting to read and follow experts who specialize in areas that you want to work on in your life.

_____

_____

_____

Some people are so much sunshine to the square inch.

WALT WHITMAN

QUICK REFERENCE

MY SUPPORTIVE COMMUNITY
Compile a list of anyone you know of who is
supportive to your better self.

People or resources that do/could help you succeed:

☐

☐

☐

☐

☐

☐

☐

☐

☐

☐

☐

☐

☐

☐

☐

☐

UPLIFTING

Quotes or mottos that help you be your best self:

"

"

"

SELF-TALK

Your words control your life, your progress, your results,
even your mental and physical health. You cannot talk
like a failure and expect to be successful.

GERMANY KENT

A human needs support from others and from themselves.
Write words of encouragement to yourself.

_____

_____

_____

_____

Why does this thing called life matter, and what do you
have to offer others? Write your personal pep talk. . .

_____

_____

_____

_____

INSPIRATIONS

Inspire others; make others believe that they can do it too. Helping others reach their dreams and get to the point in their life where they are finally happy with everything is the moment I live for.

ESHRAQ JIAD
GOING FROM NOTHING TO EVERYTHING

GET SUPPORT. LOOK TO
PEOPLE WHO HAVE GONE BEFORE
YOU FOR ENCOURAGEMENT
AND INSPIRATION.

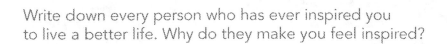

INSPIRATIONS

Write down every person who has ever inspired you
to live a better life. Why do they make you feel inspired?

How can you be an inspiration for others?

Those who bring sunshine into the lives of others
cannot keep it from themselves.

JAMES M. BARRIE

MINDSET

Let your light shine as an inspiration to humanity and
BE THE REASON someone believes in the goodness of people.

GERMANY KENT

Write down an idea that is different from how you were raised.
Make sure it is one that allows goodness and growth inside
yourself and goodness for others.

Write down all of those new ideas that you can think of.

Bring sunshine into the place you enter.

LATIKA TEOTIA

YOUR VERSION OF SUCCESS

*Define success on your own terms, achieve it by
your own rules, and build a life you're proud to live.*

ANNE SWEENEY

What does success mean to you?
Not what the world tells you success should be,
but what your heart, gut, and experience tell you.

SUCCESS MEANS . . .

Are you scared of success?   ☐ YES   ☐ NO

What limiting beliefs are holding you back
and how can you grow past those limiting beliefs?

LIMITING BELIEFS	HOW TO GROW PAST

DREAMS

Having a dream is like having sunshine. Without it, you cannot see as clear.

With it, your world shines. Have a dream, and the light will fill your eyes with hope.

J.R. RIM

EXPLORE YOUR DREAMS.
LET YOURSELF THINK ABOUT
HOW YOUR DREAM LIFE WOULD FEEL.
SOAK IN HOW IT COULD BE FULFILLING
AND BENEFICIAL TO THE WORLD.

YOUR DREAMS

Nothing happens unless we first dream.

CARL JUNG

If you could have anything in the world, what would it be?

What would your life look like both in the big picture
and in the day-to-day?

BIG PICTURE

DAY-TO-DAY

BIGGER DREAMS

We are limited, not by our abilities, but by our vision.
You gotta have a BIG vision to know what your abilities are.
Don't be afraid. Fear limits YOU and YOUR VISION.
It's okay to DREAM and dream BIG.
KEEP YOUR DREAMS ALIVE. KEEP YOURSELF ALIVE.
Don't just exist. Live. Thrive. Love. Share. Care. DARE!!

ABHISHEK KUMAR

Keep pushing yourself beyond your comfort zone.

What are bigger visions for your life?

What are bigger visions for your community?

My expanded dream:

TALENTS

What are your innate talents and strengths?	What do people come to you for help with?

What aspects of life do you enjoy, and what comes naturally to you?	What aspect of life interests you?

YOUR BEST SELF

The goal is not to be better than the other man,
but your previous self.

DALAI LAMA

Dwell on the best version of you. Dwell on the gifts that
you can contribute to the world, both big and small.

How can you be just a little bit better than you were yesterday?

_____

_____

_____

_____

_____

How could you use your unique talents to better the world,
and to get yourself closer to your dream life?

_____

_____

_____

_____

_____

YOUR FUTURE

No matter who you are, no matter what you did,
no matter where you've come from, you can always change,
become a better version of yourself.

MADONNA

Write down all of the ways you could grow.

Write down all of the ways that could add to your legacy,
in both big and small ways.

BIG WAYS	SMALL WAYS

YOUR BUCKET LIST

*The purpose of life is to live it, to taste experience
to the utmost, to reach out eagerly and without
fear for newer and richer experience.*

ELEANOR ROOSEVELT

Things I want to do before I die:

☐

☐

☐

☐

☐

☐

☐

☐

☐

☐

☐

☐

☐

☐

OUTWARD CONTRIBUTION

Only those who have learned the power of sincere and selfless contribution experience life's deepest joy: true fulfillment.

TONY ROBBINS

In what ways are you contributing to your family, neighbors, community, and world?

How could you contribute more?

What problems do you notice in the world? In what ways, big or small, could you help?

MY CONTRIBUTION BUCKET LIST
Things I want to contribute to the world before I die:

☐

☐

☐

☐

☐

☐

☐

☐

YOUR LIFE

Life is a blank canvas, and you need to
throw all the paint on it you can.

DANNY KAYE

How can you add paint to the canvas that is your life,
in either big or little ways?

What can you add to your life to enhance it?

+

+

+

+

ACTIONS

You must be the change

you wish to see in the world.

GANDHI

YOU CAN MAKE THE WORLD
A BETTER PLACE IN
YOUR OWN WAY,
IN YOUR FAMILY,
IN YOUR NEIGHBORHOOD,
IN YOUR COMMUNITY,
IN YOUR IMMEDIATE WORLD.

LIVE YOUR BEST LIFE
INTENTIONALLY

For me, I am driven by two main philosophies:
know more today about the world than I knew
yesterday and lessen the suffering of others.
You'd be surprised how far that gets you.

NEIL DEGRASSE TYSON

How can you be who you needed when you were younger?

What type of person do you wish had existed?

How can you be that person for others?

What are small daily habits that can get you where you
want to be in life?

What are big life decisions that can help you get where you
want to be in life?

WISDOM AND YOUR DREAMS

Experience is the best teacher.

JULIUS CAESAR

PUTTING YOUR BIG DREAMS IN ACTION

Try out your dreams in a small way. You will gain insight along the journey to see if that dream is a good fit for you and your life.

How can you test out one aspect of your dream this week to see if that dream is a fit for your life?

ASPECT	TEST

ACTION STEPS TO MAKE
YOUR DREAMS A REALITY

Start where you are. Use what you have. Do what you can.

ARTHUR ASHE

Make your big idea clear.
Break it into categories.
Break it into smaller actionable steps.

BIG IDEA / DREAM

*+ Complete the "Your Goal's Plan" section on the following pages
to help you turn your dreams into reality.*

YOUR GOAL'S PLAN

YOUR GOAL

YOUR PURPOSE
Why do you want to accomplish the goal?

BREAK IT DOWN into six categories!
Any six ways to help your brain organize your goal.

A	B	C
D	E	F

NEXT, break each category into actionable steps.

A

   1.

   2.

   3.

B

   1.

   2.

   3.

C

   1.

   2.

   3.

D

   1.

   2.

   3.

E

   1.

   2.

   3.

F

   1.

   2.

   3.

DEDICATED

Whether you think you can,
or you think you can't — you're right.

HENRY FORD

Have agency over your actions. Set yourself up to succeed.

Write your commitment to accomplishing your dream.

....

....

....

HOW can you set yourself up to succeed?

+

+

+

WHAT are steps to keep you accountable?

+

+

+

WHO can give you support?

+

+

+

A HEALTHY MINDSET FOR GOALS

Accomplish one step at a time.
Tweak actions as you reflect on the journey
with wisdom and patience.
Stay focused.
Stay consistent.
Give yourself time and space.
Push yourself.
Circle back to your motivation.
Keep support, purpose, and love close to you.
Evaluate your life to learn and grow.
Learn when to grow past a challenge,
when to put a plan on hold, and when it is wise to quit.

OTHER GOALS YOU HOPE TO ACCOMPLISH:

+ Additioanl "Goal Plans" pages are located in the last section of this journal.

MY WHY

REASONS I CARE ABOUT LIFE:

☐

☐

☐

☐

☐

☐

☐

☐

☐

☐

☐

☐

☐

☐

MY MOTTO

How you want to live your life. Your life motto and mantra.

LIFE INVENTORY REASSESSMENT

How would you describe these areas of your life?
Comment on your satisfaction in each box.
Which could use growth?

HAPPINESS + HOPE	RELATIONSHIPS + LOVE FOR OTHERS	CHARACTER + VIRTUE + HONOR	ADVENTURE + CURIOSITY + CHALLENGE
○ Needs Growth	○ Needs Growth	○ Needs Growth	○ Needs Growth
PURPOSE + CONTRIBUTION	PHYSICAL HEALTH	MENTAL HEALTH	SHAME + GUILT + REGRET
○ Needs Growth	○ Needs Growth	○ Needs Growth	○ Needs Growth
GROWTH + LEARNING	FINANCIAL MANAGEMENT + TIME MANAGEMENT	MATURITY + RESPONSIBILITIES	SPIRITUALITY
○ Needs Growth	○ Needs Growth	○ Needs Growth	○ Needs Growth
STRESS LEVELS	COMMUNITY + SUPPORT	BOUNDARIES	SELF-CARE + SELF-ESTEEM
○ Needs Growth	○ Needs Growth	○ Needs Growth	○ Needs Growth

EXTRA PAGES

ADDITIONAL GOAL PLANS

ADDITIONAL EMOTION PAGES

ALL ABOUT YOU PAGES

ADDITIONAL JOURNAL PROMPTS

FREE JOURNALING SPACE

YOUR GOAL'S PLAN

YOUR GOAL

YOUR PURPOSE
Why do you want to accomplish the goal?

BREAK IT DOWN into six categories!
Any six ways to help your brain organize your goal.

A	B	C

D	E	F

NEXT, break each category into actionable steps.

A
  1. ....
  2. ....
  3. ....

B
  1. ....
  2. ....
  3. ....

C
  1. ....
  2. ....
  3. ....

D
  1. ....
  2. ....
  3. ....

E
  1. ....
  2. ....
  3. ....

F
  1. ....
  2. ....
  3. ....

DEDICATED

Whether you think you can,
or you think you can't — you're right.

HENRY FORD

Have agency over your actions. Set yourself up to succeed.

Write your commitment to accomplishing your dream.

....

....

....

HOW can you set yourself up to succeed?

+

+

+

WHAT are steps to keep you accountable?

+

+

+

WHO can give you support?

+

+

+

JOURNAL

YOUR GOAL'S PLAN

YOUR GOAL

YOUR PURPOSE
Why do you want to accomplish the goal?

BREAK IT DOWN into six categories!
Any six ways to help your brain organize your goal.

A	B	C

D	E	F

NEXT, break each category into actionable steps.

A
  1.
  2.
  3.

B
  1.
  2.
  3.

C
  1.
  2.
  3.

D
  1.
  2.
  3.

E
  1.
  2.
  3.

F
  1.
  2.
  3.

DEDICATED

Whether you think you can,
or you think you can't — you're right.

HENRY FORD

Have agency over your actions. Set yourself up to succeed.

Write your commitment to accomplishing your dream.

....

....

....

HOW can you set yourself up to succeed?

+

+

+

WHAT are steps to keep you accountable?

+

+

+

WHO can give you support?

+

+

+

JOURNAL

YOUR GOAL'S PLAN

YOUR GOAL

YOUR PURPOSE
Why do you want to accomplish the goal?

BREAK IT DOWN into six categories!
Any six ways to help your brain organize your goal.

A	B	C
D	E	F

NEXT, break each category into actionable steps.

A
  1. ....
  2. ....
  3. ....

B
  1. ....
  2. ....
  3. ....

C
  1. ....
  2. ....
  3. ....

D
  1. ....
  2. ....
  3. ....

E
  1. ....
  2. ....
  3. ....

F
  1. ....
  2. ....
  3. ....

DEDICATED

Whether you think you can,
or you think you can't — you're right.

HENRY FORD

Have agency over your actions. Set yourself up to succeed.

Write your commitment to accomplishing your dream.

....

....

....

HOW can you set yourself up to succeed?

+

+

+

WHAT are steps to keep you accountable?

+

+

+

WHO can give you support?

+

+

+

JOURNAL

JOURNAL

EMOTIONS

When we understand people; when we understand situations;
when we understand what matters; when we understand
the why's, the what's and the how's; when we understand
the trigger of actions, we least inflict pain on
ourselves and unto others.

ERNEST AGYEMANG YEBOAH

Emotions educate us. Just accept the emotion.
Feel it and try to understand it.

NOTE: *For this exercise, emotions by themselves are neither good nor bad.*
What is important, is to understand why you are experiencing them, and
being able to have a healthy response and action.

PICK AN EMOTION.

sad	motivated	empty	compassionate
depressed	content	guilty	sensitive
anxious	jealous	annoyed	determined
nervous	volatile	empowered	energetic
irritated	unmotivated	supported	calm
lonely	angry	powerful	amazed
excited	deflated	happy	peaceful
hopeful	tired	grateful	inspired
joyful	fearful	confident	stable
at peace			

Response and Action on the following pages.

What happened to make you feel that way?

What were the circumstances around your situation?

What did your emotions tell you about that situation?

Did you handle your behavior in a mature way after feeling
the emotion? Why?

How can you set your life up so that you respond to triggers
in healthy ways?

What are needs that you have that this emotion is clueing
you into?

Are there any boundaries you could implement?

Are there any mentors you could talk to?

What support do you need to handle this emotion better?

What growth do you need to handle this situation better?

CONCERNING YOUR EMOTIONAL RESPONSE:
Did you do what you felt was right? What was the outcome?

To be happy, you must be your own sunshine.

C.E. JERNINGHAM

JOURNAL

EMOTIONS

When we understand people; when we understand situations;
when we understand what matters; when we understand
the why's, the what's and the how's; when we understand
the trigger of actions, we least inflict pain on
ourselves and unto others.

ERNEST AGYEMANG YEBOAH

Emotions educate us. Just accept the emotion.
Feel it and try to understand it.

NOTE: *For this exercise, emotions by themselves are neither good nor bad.*
What is important, is to understand why you are experiencing them, and
being able to have a healthy response and action.

PICK AN EMOTION.

sad	motivated	empty	compassionate
depressed	content	guilty	sensitive
anxious	jealous	annoyed	determined
nervous	volatile	empowered	energetic
irritated	unmotivated	supported	calm
lonely	angry	powerful	amazed
excited	deflated	happy	peaceful
hopeful	tired	grateful	inspired
joyful	fearful	confident	stable
at peace			

Response and Action on the following pages.

What happened to make you feel that way?

What were the circumstances around your situation?

What did your emotions tell you about that situation?

Did you handle your behavior in a mature way after feeling the emotion? Why?

How can you set your life up so that you respond to triggers in healthy ways?

What are needs that you have that this emotion is clueing you into?

Are there any boundaries you could implement?

Are there any mentors you could talk to?

What support do you need to handle this emotion better?

What growth do you need to handle this situation better?

CONCERNING YOUR EMOTIONAL RESPONSE:
Did you do what you felt was right? What was the outcome?

To be happy, you must be your own sunshine.

C.E. JERNINGHAM

JOURNAL

EMOTIONS

When we understand people; when we understand situations;
when we understand what matters; when we understand
the why's, the what's and the how's; when we understand
the trigger of actions, we least inflict pain on
ourselves and unto others.

ERNEST AGYEMANG YEBOAH

Emotions educate us. Just accept the emotion.
Feel it and try to understand it.

NOTE: *For this exercise, emotions by themselves are neither good nor bad.*
What is important, is to understand why you are experiencing them, and
being able to have a healthy response and action.

PICK AN EMOTION.

sad	motivated	empty	compassionate
depressed	content	guilty	sensitive
anxious	jealous	annoyed	determined
nervous	volatile	empowered	energetic
irritated	unmotivated	supported	calm
lonely	angry	powerful	amazed
excited	deflated	happy	peaceful
hopeful	tired	grateful	inspired
joyful	fearful	confident	stable
at peace			

Response and Action on the following pages.

What happened to make you feel that way?

What were the circumstances around your situation?

What did your emotions tell you about that situation?

Did you handle your behavior in a mature way after feeling the emotion? Why?

How can you set your life up so that you respond to triggers in healthy ways?

What are needs that you have that this emotion is clueing you into?

Are there any boundaries you could implement?

Are there any mentors you could talk to?

What support do you need to handle this emotion better?

What growth do you need to handle this situation better?

CONCERNING YOUR EMOTIONAL RESPONSE:
Did you do what you felt was right? What was the outcome?

To be happy, you must be your own sunshine.

C.E. JERNINGHAM

JOURNAL

EMOTIONS

When we understand people; when we understand situations;
when we understand what matters; when we understand
the why's, the what's and the how's; when we understand
the trigger of actions, we least inflict pain on
ourselves and unto others.

ERNEST AGYEMANG YEBOAH

Emotions educate us. Just accept the emotion.
Feel it and try to understand it.

NOTE: *For this exercise, emotions by themselves are neither good nor bad.*
What is important, is to understand why you are experiencing them, and
being able to have a healthy response and action.

PICK AN EMOTION.

sad	motivated	empty	compassionate
depressed	content	guilty	sensitive
anxious	jealous	annoyed	determined
nervous	volatile	empowered	energetic
irritated	unmotivated	supported	calm
lonely	angry	powerful	amazed
excited	deflated	happy	peaceful
hopeful	tired	grateful	inspired
joyful	fearful	confident	stable
at peace			

Response and Action on the following pages.

What happened to make you feel that way?

What were the circumstances around your situation?

What did your emotions tell you about that situation?

Did you handle your behavior in a mature way after feeling the emotion? Why?

How can you set your life up so that you respond to triggers in healthy ways?

What are needs that you have that this emotion is clueing you into?

Are there any boundaries you could implement?

Are there any mentors you could talk to?

What support do you need to handle this emotion better?

What growth do you need to handle this situation better?

CONCERNING YOUR EMOTIONAL RESPONSE:
Did you do what you felt was right? What was the outcome?

To be happy, you must be your own sunshine.

C.E. JERNINGHAM

ALL ABOUT YOU

Your preferences show your interests, your joys, and perhaps an insight into a way you could contribute to the world.

Answer these questions quickly based on instinct.

What is the most important thing in your life?

What is the biggest annoyance in your life?

What do you do well?

What could you do better?

What do you want to improve in your life?

What makes you want to keep living?

What makes you content after a long day?

What lifelong goal do you have that you are ignoring?

What is your ideal day?

What would you do with $1 million?

What makes you happy?

What makes you mad?

What makes you sad?

What three things would you wish for from a genie?

Are you happy?

Do you like your job?

Do you like what you do?

Do you like where you live?

What life change would make you happier?

What did you want to be when you were a kid?

Who are you jealous of and why?

What is your favorite hobby?

What is your favorite weekend activity?

Where would you go on an all-expenses paid vacation?

YOUR FAVORITES

Genre of music:

Song:

Artist:

Movie:

TV channel:

Show to binge:

Book:

Author:

Magazine:

Podcast:

Celebrity:

Historical figure:

Time of day/year:

Hobby:

Way to spend money:

Subject to learn:

Region:

Country:

Temperature:

Culture:

Cuisine:

Drink:

Vacation destination:

Holiday:

Material item:

Activity:

VISION BOARD

Draw or paste pictures to visualize
how you can add love to the world's story.

EXTRA PROMPTS FOR ADDITIONAL JOURNALING

Feed your soul with good things.

What are you nurturing?

Where are you stuck in life? Why do you think you are there? What reward do you still get from acting that way, even if it feels negative?

Focus on the good that you do have.

What healthy actions can you add to your life today for better mental, emotional, spiritual, physical, or financial health?

How can you prevent buildup of negative emotions?

Negotiate with your mind. What can possibly be done to get you to a better place?

YOUR LIFE TODAY

Give yourself permission to enjoy this present moment.
Resist the urge to fill it with I need to's, I shoulds, I coulds.
Trying to fill all your present moments is impeding
the natural flow of life.

NANETTE MATHEWS

Give yourself permission to be happy, both in the
big picture of your life and in the small everyday moments.

I give myself permission to be happy in the present moment and
here is why . . .

YOUR PLACE IN THIS WORLD

In what ways, big and small, can you add love to the world's story?

BIG WAYS	SMALL WAYS

JOURNAL PROMPT

The sun,--the bright sun, that brings back, not light alone,
but new life, and hope, and freshness to man--burst upon
the crowded city in clear and radiant glory.
Through costly-coloured glass and paper-mended window,
through cathedral dome and rotten crevice, it shed its equal ray.

CHARLES DICKENS

Printed in the United States
by Baker & Taylor Publisher Services